WORKBOOK 4

prepared for the course team by bob kelly

This publication forms part of an Open University course DD100 *An Introduction to the Social Sciences: Understanding Social Change*. Details of this and other Open University courses can be obtained from the Course Information and Advice Centre, PO Box 724, The Open University, Milton Keynes MK7 6ZS, United Kingdom: tel. +44 (0)1908 653231, e-mail general-enquiries@open.ac.uk

Alternatively, you may visit the Open University website at http://www.open.ac.uk where you can learn more about the wide range of courses and packs offered at all levels by The Open University.

To purchase a selection of Open University course materials visit the webshop at www.ouw.co.uk, or contact Open University Worldwide, Michael Young Building, Walton Hall, Milton Keynes MK7 6AA, United Kingdom for a brochure. tel. +44 (0)1908 858785; fax +44 (0)1908 858787; e-mail ouwenq@open.ac.uk

The Open University
Walton Hall, Milton Keynes
MK7 6AA

First published 2000. Second edition 2001. Third edition 2004

Edited, designed and typeset by The Open University.

Printed and bound in the United Kingdom by the Alden Group, Oxford

ISBN 0 7492 5366 5

3.1

B/dd100wb4isbn074925366513.1

Contents

The DD100 course team

John Allen, *Professor of Geography*

Penny Bennett, *Editor*

Pam Berry, *Compositor*

Simon Bromley, *Senior Lecturer in Government*

Lydia Chant, *Course Manager*

Stephen Clift, *Editor*

Allan Cochrane, *Professor of Public Policy*

Lene Connolly, *Print Buying Controller*

Jonathan Davies, *Graphic Designer*

Graham Dawson, *Lecturer in Economics*

Ross Fergusson, *Staff Tutor in Social Policy (Region 02)*

Fran Ford, *Senior Course Co-ordination Secretary*

Ian Fribbance, *Staff Tutor in Economics (Region 01)*

David Goldblatt, *Co-Course Team Chair*

Richard Golden, *Production and Presentation Administrator*

Jenny Gove, *Lecturer in Psychology*

Peter Hamilton, *Lecturer in Sociology*

Celia Hart, *Picture Researcher*

David Held, *Professor of Politics and Sociology*

Susan Himmelweit, *Professor of Economics*

Stephen Hinchliffe, *Lecturer in Geography*

Wendy Hollway, *Professor of Psychology*

Gordon Hughes, *Senior Lecturer in Social Policy*

Wendy Humphreys, *Staff Tutor in Government (Region 01)*

Jonathan Hunt, *Co-publishing Advisor*

Christina Janoszka, *Course Manager*

Pat Jess, *Staff Tutor in Geography (Region 12)*

Bob Kelly, *Staff Tutor in Government (Region 06)*

Margaret Kiloh, *Staff Tutor in Social Policy (Region 13)*

Sylvia Lay-Flurrie, *Secretary*

Gail Lewis, *Senior Lecturer in Social Policy*

Siân Lewis, *Graphic Designer*

Liz McFall, *Lecturer in Sociology*

Tony McGrew, *Professor of International Relations, University of Southampton*

Hugh Mackay, *Staff Tutor in Sociology (Region 10)*

Maureen Mackintosh, *Professor of Economics*

Eugene McLaughlin, *Senior Lecturer in Criminology and Social Policy*

Andrew Metcalf, *Senior Producer, BBC*

Gerry Mooney, *Staff Tutor in Social Policy (Region 11)*

Lesley Moore, *Senior Course Co-ordination Secretary*

Ray Munns, *Graphic Artist*

Karim Murji, *Senior Lecturer in Sociology*

Sarah Neal, *Lecturer in Social Policy*

Kathy Pain, *Staff Tutor in Geography (Region 02)*

Clive Pearson, *Tutor Panel*

Ann Phoenix, *Professor of Psychology*

Lynn Poole, *Tutor Panel*

Raia Prokhovnik, *Senior Lecturer in Government*

Norma Sherratt, *Staff Tutor in Sociology (Region 03)*

Roberto Simonetti, *Lecturer in Economics*

Dick Skellington, *Project Officer*

Brenda Smith, *Staff Tutor in Psychology (Region 12)*

Mark Smith, *Senior Lecturer in Government*

Matt Staples, *Course Manager*

Grahame Thompson, *Professor of Political Economy*

Ken Thompson, *Professor of Sociology*

Diane Watson, *Staff Tutor in Sociology (Region 05)*

Stuart Watt, *Lecturer in Psychology*

Andy Whitehead, *Graphic Artist*

Kath Woodward, *Course Team Chair, Senior Lecturer in Sociology*

Chris Wooldridge, *Editor*

External Assessor

Nigel Thrift, *Professor of Geography, University of Oxford*

INTRODUCTION

Welcome to Block 4 of the course, on which you will be working for the next five weeks. The workbook will again be your guide through your studies. Before you begin work on Book 4 and the other course materials there are several important matters that we need to bring to your attention.

Block overview

As with the earlier blocks of study, Block 4 combines a range of teaching materials, the textbook *A Globalizing World? Culture, Economics, Politics*, two audio-cassettes, a study skills supplement on reading maps, a TV programme, and this workbook. The recommended study timetable and path through this are shown in Figures 1 and 2.

Study week	Course material	Suggested study time
21	*Workbook 4* and Book 4: *A Globalizing World? Culture,* *Economics, Politics* Introduction Chapter 1 Audio-cassette 7, Side A and notes	11 hours 1 hour
22	Workbook and Chapter 2 Audio-cassette 7, Side B and notes	11 hours 1 hour
23	Workbook and Chapter 3 Audio-cassette 8, Side A and notes	10 hours 2 hours
24	Workbook, Chapter 4 and Afterword *Study Skills Supplement 3: Reading Maps* plus Audio-cassette 8, Side B TV 04 and notes	10 hours 1 hour 1 hour
25	TMA 04	12 hours

FIGURE 1   Course materials for Block 4

FIGURE 2 Recommended study route for Block 4

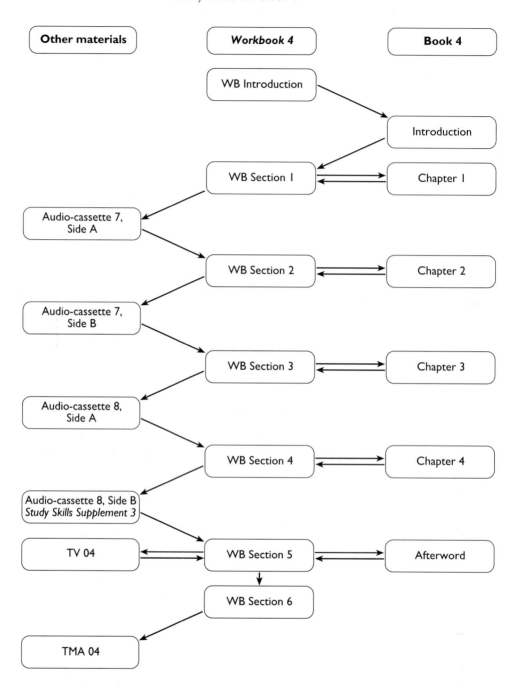

Block 4 presents a shift in direction on DD100, both in terms of the key questions which focus on the global arena and the UK's place in the world, and in our development of the circuit of knowledge, to focus on different *theories* of how knowledge is produced. You have met different claims which use evidence to support particular theoretical positions before in DD100. In Block 4 we take the focus on theories further and work on developing the

very important skills which will enable you to evaluate different theories in the social sciences by means of tests to weigh up their strengths and weaknesses that we introduced in *Looking Back and Moving On: Writing Essays and Evaluating Theories Booklet.*

Key questions

In this block the focus of attention switches. Most of the course, so far, has studied the UK state, economy and society. Block 4 looks at the global and the United Kingdom's place in the world. It asks what impact changing information systems and patterns of world trade have on individual states such as the UK, and whether these states and societies can still determine their own policies and priorities. We have broken down these issues into four key questions that run throughout Block 4.

1 What is globalization?

A range of evidence suggests that events in other parts of the world continually affect our lives; for example: problems of environmental pollution, the activities of foreign-owned corporations, or wars between and within other states. But how should we best describe or conceptualize globalization? What areas of social life does it apply to?

2 How significant is contemporary globalization?

A quick glance at the historical record suggests that long-distance and socially-significant interactions between societies are hardly new. Islam, in the space of a few centuries, had spread from its Arabian heartland to Spain in the West and northern India in the East, transforming religious, cultural and political life in every society along the way. Moreover, complex and intense long-distance relationships of trade, pilgrimage and military alliance across the Islamic lands meant that a high level of interaction was maintained. Closer to the present, the late nineteenth century saw an enormous expansion of global military, economic and political interconnections as European empires stretched to every continent. So is there anything distinctively new about contemporary forms of globalization? Is it the sheer quantity and speed of global interactions that differentiates the present from the past? Is the geography of interaction different?

3 What is the impact of globalization on the sovereignty and autonomy of nation-states?

Look at a map of the world today and it is almost entirely carved up into separate, bordered nation-states. Within each of these territorially demarcated areas, the state claims to be *sovereign*; that it above all possesses exclusive and rightful jurisdiction as the highest legal authority in the land. Moreover, sovereign states claim to be able to shape practically the destinies of their citizens, independently of outside forces, and thus possess *autonomy*. But in a world where states have signed up to all kinds of global legal documents, human rights charters and international organizations, what is left of their individual sovereignty? More to the point, in a world where drugs and money cross borders with impunity, can a single nation-state really solve its own drug problems or regulate its economy by itself? If governments can't automatically control these things, can anyone or any organization? If someone or a body has such control, is there any democratic accountability?

4   Are there winners and losers in globalization?

How are the costs and benefits of social change triggered by globalization distributed? Does the global economy, for example, enrich some at the expense of others? Within the UK, are some classes and regions benefiting from free trade and global financial deregulation and others suffering? Is there a substantial argument that women are being particularly exploited and disadvantaged by global developments? Across the world, how do these 'goods' and 'bads' get distributed? Are there some social groups or whole societies who are not even part of global networks?

Alongside these four questions, we will also be asking you to think through and try to reframe these issues in terms of the course themes. One way of thinking this through for *uncertainty and diversity* and *structure and agency* would be:

- To what extent does globalization create a more uncertain environment for individual societies and states?

- Does global interconnectedness and access to the global flow of ideas and cultures encourage greater diversity within societies? Can it lead to a greater resistance to outside influences? Does it lead to the creation of a bland and uniform global culture?

- To what extent do global structures – supranational institutions, global flows of information, patterns of global trade and investment – shape and constrain the agency of individuals, firms and governments? What opportunities does globalization create?

The role of changing flows and forms of knowledge and information is also a feature of this block. We want you to focus on the analytical strand of *knowledge and knowing* in this block and to do so as part of the key skills work.

Key skills

Evaluating social science claims and theories

In earlier chapters of this course you have met a range of theories which attempt to explain a whole variety of types of individual behaviour and patterns of social change: the causes of crime, the origins of nationalism, the creation of human intelligence, etc.

Moreover, you will have often found that we have presented more than one theoretical explanation of crime or nationalism. The questions will have certainly occurred to you, which theory is stronger?, or more valuable?, or more accurate? Answering these questions draws on the process of *evaluation*; it is the key skill that this block works on and forms the final element of the circuit of knowledge (Figure 3).

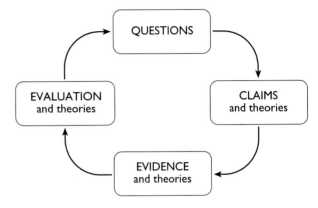

FIGURE 3   The circuit of knowledge

Evaluating *claims* and *theories* in the social sciences is a complex and much contested terrain, as you have seen in *Looking Back and Moving On: Writing Essays and Evaluating Theories Booklet.* In DD100 we have chosen to use three *tests* as our tools of evaluation. Simply put, those tests are:

- Is the claim or theory *coherent*?

- How well does the claim or theory account for *empirical evidence*?

- How *comprehensive* an explanation does the claim or theory generate?

For shorthand purposes we will call these tests of evaluation: *coherence*, *empirical adequacy*, and *comprehensiveness*.

Coherence

In general there are three ways of testing the coherence of a claim or theory. First, we can look at the clarity of the key claims and concepts. Second, we can look at how logical the links are in the chain of reasoning that makes up the theory. Third, we can examine the plausibility and accuracy of the often unspoken or hidden assumptions that those concepts and chains of reasoning rest upon.

In *Looking Back and Moving On: Writing Essays and Evaluating Theories Booklet* we showed you how to apply this and the other tests to theories about crime. Here let us look at the claim of the liberal political tradition which you encountered in Block 3, that *democracy is good for economic growth*.

How could we begin to test the coherence of this claim?

In terms of *conceptual clarity* we might ask what precisely is meant by the key terms. Democracy comes in many forms and many shades of grey, so what exactly are the criteria for saying whether a society is democratic or authoritarian? Do societies have to possess all the features of democracy, such as universal suffrage, to generate economic growth or just some, such as the rule of law? And what is meant by good here? – a sharper description of the causal relationship between democratic politics and economic growth is required.

This could take us to the *chain of reasoning*. To really explore this we would need to know a lot more about the details of the liberal argument than support the claim we have been looking at. One version of the chain of reasoning might look like this:

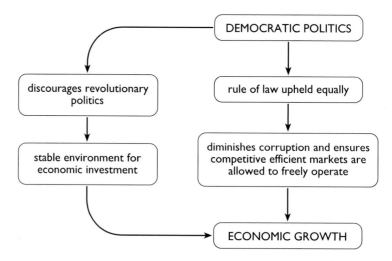

Pressing this further in terms of its *chain of reasoning* and *unspoken assumptions* we could ask:

- Why does democratic politics discourage revolutionary politics? Doesn't authoritarian politics do the same? Could we argue that oppression can also deter possible opposition?

- Is the rule of law the only or the main reason for diminishing corruption? Do organizational systems and practices prevent or deter corruption? Do particular cultures encourage or discourage corruption?

- A key assumption buried in this chain of reasoning concerns the relationship between free markets and growth. Are free markets the main source of economic growth? If so, why?

Empirical adequacy

As we have argued throughout DD100, gathering and organizing empirical evidence is only one step in the circuit of knowledge – you have to do something with it. That something is an essential element of the process of evaluation. Tests of *empirical adequacy* – how claims and theories fare when actually faced with information about the world – fall into a number of categories.

First, evidence may support or *verify* a theory. To continue with our example, if a theory claims that democracy is good for economic growth, then evidence of countries with democratic politics and high rates of economic growth would help verify the theory. However, evidence may also refute or *falsify* a theory.

What sort of evidence would falsify our theory about democracy and economic growth?

Examples would include authoritarian societies with high rates of economic growth (such as South Korea in the 1970s or China in the 1990s) or democratic societies with low rates of economic growth (such as the UK in the 1970s or Germany in the 1990s).

Comprehensiveness

The test of *comprehensiveness* can also be understood in a number of different ways. First we can ask how broad the coverage of a theory is in time and space. Does the liberal theory of the relationship between democracy and economic growth stand for all types of societies and all historical periods or just some? The rather awkward cases of authoritarian East Asian societies with high rates of growth could be explained away by restricting the comprehensiveness of the theory to European and North American societies. Even then it might be in trouble when looking at the case of pre-First World War Germany (rapid growth and limited democratic politics).

Another test of comprehensiveness would be how many facets of social life a theory incorporates. In the case of democracy and economic growth, the liberal theory is quite narrow. It does not take into account the possibilities that specifically economic or cultural structures, or even wider global conditions, might shape economic growth. Of course, a more elaborate, comprehensive account of economic growth has been constructed by liberals from the crude model presented here.

- The key skill developed in Block 4 is *evaluating* claims and theories; weighing up their strengths and weaknesses.
- Evaluating can be based on three tests: *coherence, empirical adequacy* and *comprehensiveness.*
- The test of coherence includes examining the clarity of concepts, the logic of the links between them, and the unspoken assumptions that underpin them.
- The test of empirical adequacy leads to verification or falsification of a theory.
- The test of comprehensiveness asks about the spatial and temporal scope of a theory and its internal complexity.

Having subjected theories to these tests, a question of comparison remains. We might find that one theory stands up well to empirical evidence but is hopelessly narrow and incomprehensive in its coverage. Should we prefer this to a theory that stands up to the evidence less well, but offered itself up to the possibility of falsification by being much more bold, complex and comprehensive in the type of argument it sought to make? What if, in both cases, the theories possessed clear flaws in the chain of reasoning or implausible assumptions about the world? Do they become useless? We will return to some of these issues in Section 5 of the workbook. However, what is certain is that a new set of unexpected *questions* will have been raised that require further investigation.

Assessing Block 4

The pattern for this block is the same as for Blocks 1 and 2 in that the fifth week of work is devoted to the production of an assignment (TMA 04) to send to your tutor. The assignment will take the form of a 1,500 word essay which will ask you to evaluate a theory or theories of globalization.

In Section 6 of this workbook we will set a 'mock' assignment that will be similar to the actual one you will face, and we will give you some guidance on how to tackle it. Our aim here is to give you a grounding in the skill of evaluation and to encourage you to think about it as you work your way through the course material.

 Now please read the Introduction to Book 4, *A Globalizing World?* Then return to this point in the workbook.

1 A GLOBALIZING SOCIETY?

So what is *globalization?* How significant is it? How does it affect our lives? How do social scientists interpret it and evaluate it? Each chapter of *A Globalizing World?* will focus on a particular dimension of globalization to illustrate these issues and debates, with authors consciously emphasizing different approaches to the topic.

In Chapter 1 we will be introducing you to three basic interpretations of global developments that we broadly classify as the views of *globalists, inter-nationalists* and *transformationalists.* The general characteristics of each of these approaches are laid out in Chapter 1, but it does need to be pointed out that we have simplified a vast array of complex material into three apparently distinct groupings. Each approach can be further sub-divided, and there is plenty of interweaving and overlap between the approaches. Our aim has not been to distort the arguments, but simply to present them in an accessible manner which enables you to engage in the important tasks of understanding, analysing and evaluating contrasting positions. If and when you go on to study further courses in the social sciences, the greater richness and complexity of these debates will be revealed.

Before we launch you into the actual debates, we want you to consider some of your own experiences and views on the relevant issues.

To begin with, let's accept for now the idea that the world is becoming a *smaller* place, that distances and the time taken to travel them have shrunk, and that what happens in your locality and the country in general is now greatly affected by what goes on in other parts of the globe.

WORKBOOK ACTIVITY 1.1

Just take a couple of minutes on this. Make a list of specific examples of the world 'becoming smaller' that you have experienced or read about which make life different now from, say, 20 or 30 years ago.

COMMENT

We won't give you our own specific answers to this as it is *your view* and experiences that matter. We can imagine a range of very different answers and examples that you may have come up with, *but we are confident that you will have found it quite easy to think of examples.*

It is important to consider cultural, economic and political dimensions of globalization and the possible relationships between them.

Try to identify the possible role of each of these dimensions in relation to these questions:

- Why do we now buy so much more imported food than in the past?

- Why are particular factories/businesses opening and closing?

- Why is there so much international news in the press and on television?

Do bear these questions in mind when you read the debates that follow – if 'globalization' really is occurring then it must have effects for all of us that are experienced in everyday situations, and it is important to understand both its causes and its effects.

The first chapter of Book 4 will introduce you to many of the key terms and theories that surround questions of globalization to set up debates that will reoccur in different forms throughout the book. It will also present you with indicators that offer ways of testing the accuracy and relevance of the competing theories, including quantitative and qualitative evidence.

KEY TASKS

Chapter 1, 'A Globalizing Society?'

- To understand the general concept of globalization.

- To be able to distinguish the theoretical approaches associated with *globalists*, *inter-nationalists* and *transformationalists*, and be able to compare and contrast them.

- To understand the range of evidence which can be drawn upon to evaluate competing theories.

 Now please read Chapter 1 and then return here. As usual you should spend about two-thirds of your time on the chapter and around one-third on this section of the workbook.

1.1 Extracting the key points from Chapter 1

If you have been following the advice given in earlier workbooks your approach to reading and understanding the chapter will have probably been:

- to skim read the chapter, taking particular note of headings, summaries, etc.;

- to remind yourself of points raised in the book Introduction and earlier parts of the workbook as to what the key questions and issues of the chapter will be; and

- to actively read the chapter, taking brief notes/highlighting points as appropriate in one or more of the ways that you feel most helpful.

If you have been able to do all this you may find that some of the activities that follow have already been completed to your satisfaction.

The key role of Chapter 1 was to open up the concept of *globalization* and the various interpretations and assessments of it.

WORKBOOK ACTIVITY 1.2

Skim your own notes on Chapter 1. How could you present them concisely to summarize the chapter at a glance?

C O M M E N T

Our notes looked like this.

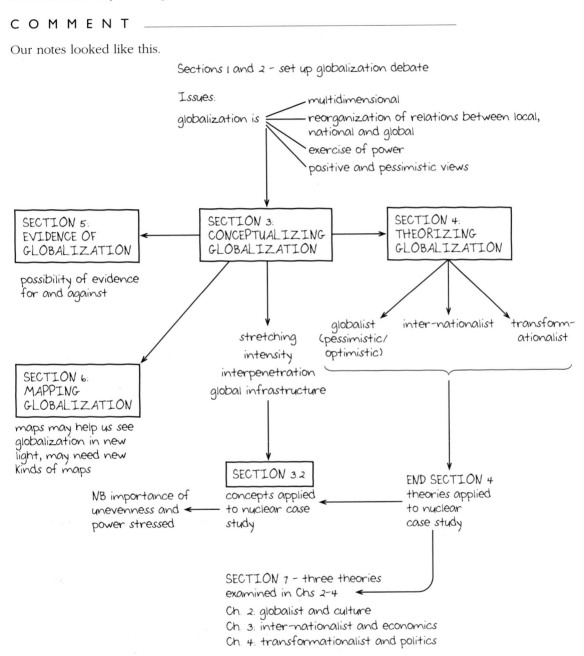

If this is the basic skeleton of the chapter, how will you be able to use and develop the material here?

● In Section 1.2 of the workbook you will be looking at concepts of globalization and evidence for globalization.

- In Section 1.3 you will be looking in more detail at the theories of globalization.

- The material on mapping globalization will be returned to in connection with *Study Skills Supplement 3: Reading Maps* (which you will be studying in week 24).

Now we want you to take another look at the material in Section 2.2 of Chapter 1 and reframe it in terms of two of the course themes. Then we will reflect on your understanding of some of the terms raised in the chapter.

WORKBOOK ACTIVITY 1.3

Look back at Readings 1.1 (Will Hutton), 1.2 (Geoff Mulgan) and 1.4 (Anthony Giddens) of Chapter 1. To what extent and in what way does the account of globalization in each extract:

- connect globalization to *uncertainty*?

- connect globalization to an increase or decrease in *diversity*?

- think about globalization in terms of *structure* and *agency*?

COMMENT

Reading 1.1: Will Hutton

Strongly suggests that globalization superficially increases diversity due to the diffusion of global brands. The English language diminishes diversity as everywhere becomes the same.

Reading 1.2: Geoff Mulgan

Mulgan notes differences between rich and poor in the face of globalization, suggesting increasing diversity and fragmentation. This account of connectedness suggests the structural impact of distant decisions without specifying the impact.

Reading 1.4: Anthony Giddens

This piece explains diversity as fragmentation and touches on the different impacts of globalization on rich and poor.

WORKBOOK ACTIVITY 1.4

As a way of checking your understanding of terms and issues raised in this chapter, try to write brief notes on the following before checking your answers in the text.

The pessimistic view of globalization

Regionalization

Global infrastructure.

COMMENT

Discussions of these terms can be found in the chapter as follows: pessimistic view, p.22; regionalization, p.15; and global infrastructure, p.17.

Use this as an opportunity to reflect on how you got on and your reactions to the activity. It is quite possible that you felt rather irritated because you couldn't answer the question or that you tried but came up with wrong answers. This is particularly irritating if you believed you had read the chapter with interest and had generally understood what it was all about. Many people will be in the same position as yourself. Treat this as a learning process. You may need to think carefully about meaning as you are reading material and to *reflect* on what you are reading to ensure it makes sense to you.

After you have read a section in a chapter do spend a few minutes trying to recall the essentials of what it said; a few minutes active thinking in this way can save you hours of reading later when you come to revise material for assignments or (in later courses) examinations.

1.2 Globalization: concepts and evidence

In Section 3.1 of the chapter, Allan Cochrane and Kathy Pain specify four distinctive features of globalization. This is very important because it presents us with a list against which examples of globalization can be checked.

The four features identified were:

- *stretched* social relations
- *intensification* of flows and interactions
- *interpenetration* of global and local social processes
- the development of a transnational *infrastructure*.

These can be difficult concepts to grasp, but they are very important for your work in this block and so now is the best time to make sure that you fully understand them.

WORKBOOK ACTIVITY 1.5

In order to pick out the key features we have completed the following grid. Our version is on page 20. We've used Sections 3 and 5 from the chapter to fill in the first two columns and in order to focus on areas of doubt we thought of some counter arguments that indicate the world is becoming globalized. We also think that there are doubts about some of the evidence which has been put forward in support of the globalization argument.

We've included blank grids for you to have a go yourself before you have a look at our version, but don't worry if you prefer to go straight to the completed grid. See if you agree with our version.

	Meaning	Evidence	Areas of doubt
Stretched relations			
Intensification			

	Meaning	Evidence	Areas of doubt
Interpenetration			
Infrastructure			

COMMENT

Our completed grid is as follows.

	Meaning	Evidence	Areas of doubt
Stretched relations	Connections to and impact on distant places.	Examples of global pollution. More countries involved in international trade. Impact of communities in creating new shared social space.	Many people in developed countries still subsistence farmers. Internet usage, etc. still internationally patchy. Regionalization may be more important (EU, etc.).
Intensification	Fast speed of links and impact.	Rapid increase of electronic flows – satellite etc. Growth in international information.	Still do not directly involve most people, even in 'developed' world.
Interpenetration	Integration of local places – local affects global and vice versa.	Global role of Microsoft, McDonald's. 'Indian' restaurants in Britain. Brazilian soaps on Portuguese TV.	Do these seriously affect people's lives? Are they just added on to traditional routine?
Infrastructure	Old state controls no longer relevant or effective.	Role of new information and new technology.	Could states reassert control if they wished?

1.3 Theories of globalization

Section 4 of Chapter 1 introduced you to the three key positions in social science debates on globalization.

The debates over the significance of globalization will be developed in the other chapters of the book; each chapter will focus on a particular subject – culture and communications, the economy, and politics. And the authors of each chapter will be stressing different interpretations of globalization. Hugh Mackay will generally stress the globalist position (Chapter 2), Bob Kelly and Raia Prokhovnik the inter-nationalist view (Chapter 3), and Anthony McGrew the transformationalist interpretation (Chapter 4).

However, to make the most of those chapters you need to establish a solid foundation of understanding now.

WORKBOOK ACTIVITY 1.6

Look back to your notes on Section 4 of Chapter 1 and try filling in the grid below which draws on our four key questions. For each question, what view does a globalist, an inter-nationalist, and a transformationalist take?

	Globalists	Inter-nationalists	Transformationalists
What is globalization?			
How significant is contemporary globalization?			

	Globalists	Inter-nationalists	Transformationalists
What is the impact of globalization on the sovereignty and autonomy of nation-states?			
Are there winners and losers in globalization?			

COMMENT

	Globalists	Inter-nationalists	Transformationalists
What is globalization?	Real and tangible shift with social processes operating on a global level. An inevitable pattern producing a single global culture and economy, and reducing state sovereignty and autonomy.	An account that tends to ignore continuities with the past. It fails to recognize scope for state sovereignty and autonomy, and that most international economic and social activity is regional rather than global.	Globalization is a complex, diverse and unpredictable process which certainly has important effects but does not remove the scope of states for independent action.
How significant is contemporary globalization?	Very significant and far-reaching.	No fundamental changes are taking place.	Significant but patchy and difficult to quantify.
What is the impact of globalization on the sovereignty and autonomy of nation-states?	State sovereignty and autonomy are disappearing with a new global structure dominating.	States remain able to determine their own priorities and systems of governance.	States remain powerful but have to adjust their role in the face of new global corporations, etc.
Are there winners and losers in globalization?	Positive globalists see the potential for all to benefit from an improved quality of life. Pessimistic globalists see dominant groups imposing their agendas and interests on the rest.	A danger of global business imposing its priorities and increasing global inequalities – the weak and poor could lose further ground to the rich and powerful.	Some scope for all to benefit from a more democratic system of governance, but the unpredictability of the process could result in a complex pattern of winners and losers.

 Now please listen to Audio-cassette 7, Side A and read the associated notes. Then return to this point in the workbook.

2 THE GLOBALIZATION OF CULTURE?

Chapter 1 of *A Globalizing World?* introduced you to the key concepts for defining globalization and the key theories that try and explain its origins and consequences. The chapter also looked at the range of evidence we might use to evaluate these theories. Chapter 2 draws upon all of this but focuses on one area of social life – culture and communications. Within this enormous field its main concern is with television, although it draws on other cultural flows as well. Three core sections (Sections 2–4) look at how each of the positions on globalization interpret the impact of global flows of television on national and local cultures, government and policy making, and local and national identities. A range of different types of evidence is drawn upon in exploring these arguments and provides a good opportunity for practising the skills of handling and evaluating evidence which builds on the skills work in *Workbook 2* and *Study Skills Supplement 2: Reading Evidence.*

The chapter combines discussion of technologies (TV transmission systems) with cultural products (TV programmes) and concludes by looking at the relative importance of technologies and cultural products in shaping and determining the impact of globalization.

KEY TASKS

Chapter 2, 'The Globalization of Culture?'

- Understanding how our concepts of globalization can be applied to cultures and cultural flows.

- Understanding what account the three theories of globalization give of cultural change.

- Beginning to compare, contrast and evaluate the three accounts.

- Working on the presentation and handling of evidence.

- Exploring the *coherence* of theoretical arguments.

- Locating theories of globalization within larger political ideologies.

Now please read Chapter 2, 'The Globalization of Culture?' and then return to this point in the workbook. You should spend two-thirds of your time on the chapter and one-third on the workbook.

2.1 Extracting the key points from Chapter 2

The chapter stresses what it calls the 'phenomenal growth in the global circulation ... of cultural goods' over recent decades, offering data on:

- the extent of cultural imports and exports,
- the growth in ownership of TV receivers and radios, and
- the expansion in the number of television channels, cable and satellite broadcasting.

The key, however, is how these developments are interpreted, and Hugh Mackay summarizes the interpretations of the *positive* and *pessimistic globalizers*, the *inter-nationalists* and the *transformationalists*.

WORKBOOK ACTIVITY 2.1

If you have already made notes on the views of *optimistic globalists* and *pessimistic globalists* then compare them with ours. If not, put down, side-by-side, notes on the points raised by each of them.

Optimistic globalists	Pessimistic globalists

COMMENT _____

Our notes were as follows (as with all notes we would, in practice, have used shorthand and abbreviations).

Optimistic globalists	Pessimistic globalists
The idea of a 'global village' – allowing communities to develop across physical boundaries – McLuhan. Democratic and participatory nature of the Internet. Space free from state control – this counters the powers of advertising, PR, etc. – Rheingold – now many voices can be heard. Use of Internet by opponents of a political system, minority ethnic group, etc. gives consumers freedom of choice.	Growing inequalities – many people do not have access to information and communications. Media increasingly owned by fewer people, e.g. Murdoch – anti-democratic potential. Lower quality programming to cater for mass audience. Internet likely to develop in ways that suit major corporations. Cultural imperialism – threat to vulnerable cultures – dominance of US culture – Frankfurt School.

Note that we have included several names of theorists who have expressed particular views (e.g. McLuhan) and examples to illustrate points (e.g. Murdoch) for use in supporting arguments in an essay. An alternative would have been to put a page reference to the chapter so that we could look up the particular example/reference when needed.

WORKBOOK ACTIVITY 2.2

Now read through your notes on Sections 3 and 4 which cover the inter-nationalists and the transformationalists. Make a list of the key points of the *transformationalist* view in a 'bullet point' format. We will do this for the inter-nationalists.

COMMENT _____

Our key points of the *inter-nationalist* view:

- do accept some changes have taken place
- believe claims excessive with key cultural forms and institutions still national

- globalists overstate external structural forces vs. local dynamics
- BBC still more viewers than satellite and cable
- very little 'truly global' TV – MTV and Disney
- 1997 top 40 programmes in UK all domestically produced
- BSkyB in many ways a UK company
- globally, broadcast material which is domestically produced is 29 times greater than cross-border (O'Regan)
- UK press essentially domestically produced
- CNN has limited significance as a broadcaster
- still significant state means of regulation, e.g. 1990 Broadcasting Act.

There is a difficult balance to be drawn between brevity and full use of examples. Here we have reminders of prominent examples, but also we have made notes from material in the order in which it was presented in the chapter; we know just where to look up further examples if needed.

Now let's use these short notes and our readings to try and summarize the arguments of the chapter based on our four block questions.

WORKBOOK ACTIVITY 2.3

Try filling in the grid below and compare it with ours.

	Optimistic globalists	Pessimistic globalists	Inter-nationalists	Transformationalists
What is cultural globalization?				
How significant is contemporary cultural globalization?				
What is the impact on national cultures, identities and politics?				

	Optimistic globalists	Pessimistic globalists	Inter-nationalists	Transformationalists
Are there winners and losers in cultural globalization?				
Evidence used.				

C O M M E N T

	Optimistic globalists	Pessimistic globalists	Inter-nationalists	Transformationalists
What is cultural globalization?	The creation of new opportunities for people to participate in the free exchange of ideas and information, free from state control.	The concentration of the power to spread ideas into the hands of a few global corporations or dominant groups who can swamp minority cultures.	There is the potential for ideas and information to spread globally, but the nation-state remains the main regulatory body and the national press and TV remains dominant.	Global cultural flows are increasing but their actual significance is difficult to measure.
How significant is contemporary cultural globalization?	Highly significant.	Highly significant.	Of little significance.	Potentially significant but unpredictable and requiring further study.
What is the impact on national cultures, identities and politics?	Enriching and democratizing.	Swamping minority cultures and homogenizing.	Marginal and peripheral.	Potentially significant but variable and unpredictable.
Are there winners and losers in cultural globalization?	Potentially all are winners.	Global corporations and dominant Western cultures are the winners, while minority cultures are the losers.	The weak are potentially the losers if pressure towards globalization is not checked.	The pattern is complex but there is scope for cultural minorities within nation-states to benefit.
Evidence used.	Quantitative data on information flows. Qualitative interpretations on use made of the Internet, etc.	Data on patterns of ownership of the media. Data on patterns of cultural flows.	Quantitative data on audience share, patterns of readership. Historical evidence of effects of the telegraph.	Data on programme content. Qualitative evidence of the active role of recipients of messages

2.2 Examining the coherence of an argument

Now let's look at Section 5 of the chapter where Hugh Mackay explores the role of technology as a factor in social change. His argument is that new technologies are key components of cultural globalization but claims their impact is gradual rather than revolutionary and that while technologies constrain societies they are themselves shaped by society.

WORKBOOK ACTIVITY 2.4

Read through Section 5 and make notes on how he develops this argument.

COMMENT

The key points we noted were:

- the telegraph greatly increased the speed of communication
- this led to cable laying, international hysteria and honours for its inventor
- claims of its impact were excessive – world peace, etc.
- terms like *stone age, steam age* stress the effects of technology, but the impact of technology depends on how technology is used
- change as a result of social concerns, etc. – the perceived needs of the US Department of Defence.

In diagrammatic form his argument can be represented thus:

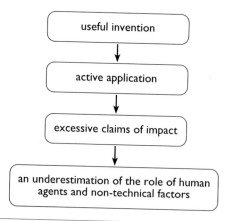

useful invention

↓

active application

↓

excessive claims of impact

↓

an underestimation of the role of human agents and non-technical factors

WORKBOOK ACTIVITY 2.5

The way Hugh Mackay presents this argument is coherent based on relevant facts and seems to be comprehensive in its coverage. Put yourself in the role of a critic, however, and see if you can identify any doubts or raise possible questions of his interpretation. Make a list of these for further consideration.

COMMENT _____

This is not an easy exercise, and doubtless Hugh Mackay would, if asked, present further justification of his views. However, we did note the following:

- He argues that the telegraph, not the Internet, was the real cause of the shrinking of time and space, but he then uses it to argue that claims about the telegraph were overblown. Could the logic of this chain of argument be questioned?

- Is there a precise parallel between the telegraph and the Internet? Could it be argued that many more people have got immediate access to the Internet than they did to the telegraph and therefore the speed of impact is likely to be different? Does the theory contain an unsustainable assumption? Has a possible line of reasoning been excluded without adequate consideration?

- Does the approach sufficiently take into account the argument that technologies may be social in their origin but can develop a momentum of their own?

Note that these points are not designed to dismiss Mackay's position, but merely to show that it is possible to raise questions and doubts about what appears a very persuasive argument.

2.3 Reading quantitative and diagrammatic evidence

One of the skills we want you to work on at this stage of the course is the critical evaluation of quantitative data, a great deal of which has been used in Chapter 2. The comments and activities here are designed to build on *Study Skills Supplement 2: Reading Evidence* and you may find it helpful to refer back to this now before proceeding with this workbook.

As we agreed in our discussion of crime in the Introductory Block, any set of statistics or tables of information have been compiled by people or institutions who may consciously or unconsciously ask questions, categorize responses/information, etc. into preconceived categories that may provide a partial or distorted picture of the world. It is therefore always important to note the sources of evidence and to consider whether the compiler or publisher might have some vested interest in the interpretations that can be drawn from the evidence; for example, the press in selling newspapers through sensationalism or politicians in showing the apparent effectiveness of their actions/policies.

Here the questions we want you to consider are rather different.

WORKBOOK ACTIVITY 2.6

Look again at Table 2.3 in the chapter which gives you information on changing patterns of television ownership in different nation-states. Try to identify and note significant information that the table does and does not tell you.

Think what extra information you would require before you could draw any conclusions about the impact of TV ownership on societies.

COMMENT

We will simply ask some questions to help you shape your answer:

- Does the extent of choice of channels matter?
- Is the source of programmes important?
- What alternatives are there to TV as cultural influences?
- How much time do people spend watching TV?

WORKBOOK ACTIVITY 2.7

Figure 4 shows exactly the same information that is presented in Table 2.3. By comparing the table with the figure we hope you can see the value of presenting evidence in different forms. Examine these two forms of presentation of data and make brief notes in answer to the question:

Do *you* think the key points can be more easily drawn from the figure or the table? In what ways?

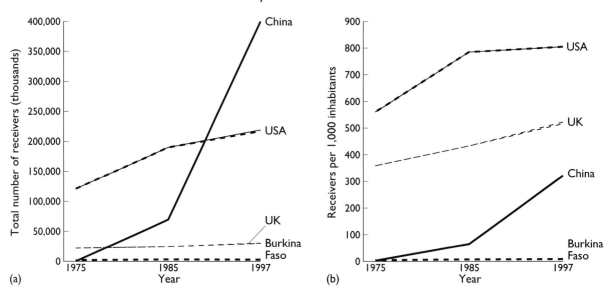

FIGURE 4   Television ownership and saturation in selected countries, 1975–97: (a) total number of receivers and (b) receivers per 1,000 inhabitants

Source: data in Table 2.3

C O M M E N T

Our thoughts are:

- Tables of numbers can appear to be complicated and rather off-putting.
- The figure helps you home in on the key point of the great increase of TV receivers in China but also that the number of receivers per 1,000 inhabitants in China is still, in 1997, considerably lower than in the USA.
- It is easier to obtain *precise* information from the table.

Whatever your reactions to this comparison it is always a useful exercise to test them against another example to see if this confirms them.

WORKBOOK ACTIVITY 2.8

Table 2.5 in the chapter gives information on the share of viewing time for public television corporations. Figure 5 shows the same information that is presented in the table. Compare Table 2.5 with Figure 5 and see if your reactions from the previous activity are confirmed.

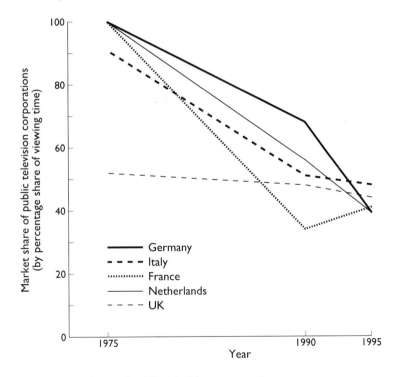

FIGURE 5   Market share of public television corporations
Source: data in Table 2.5

COMMENT

In this case we would suggest the points about relative clarity of message and the ability to produce precise statistics are even more justified, thus emphasizing the potential trade-off between the two requirements if only one form of presentation of data is to be used.

2.4 Theories of globalization and political ideologies

In Block 3 you were introduced to the key political ideologies of the post-Second World War UK. In Chapter 2, Hugh Mackay outlines a number of different views of global culture and communications under the headings of positive globalists, pessimistic globalists, traditionalists, and transformationalists. Is there any overlap? This section provides an opportunity for you to practise ideology-spotting skills.

WORKBOOK ACTIVITY 2.9

Look back at the material in Book 3 on Marxism and liberalism to remind yourself of their key assumptions (Chapter 4, Sections 3.1 and 3.3). Then look again at your notes on the sections of Hugh Mackay's chapter that cover theories of globalization and see if you can identify any links between them.

Do this by completing the following grid. You may well find that parts of the grid will remain blank.

	Marxism	Liberalism
Positive globalists		

	Marxism	Liberalism
Pessimistic globalists		
Inter-nationalists		
Transformationalists		

COMMENT

	Marxism	Liberalism
Positive globalists		Belief in the value of the free market. Value free choice and diversity.
Pessimistic globalists	Growing inequalities within and between nations. Concentration of ownership – power of wealthy people and organizations. 'Western cultural imperialism' – to generate demand for goods.	
Inter-nationalists	Traditional patterns of power and inequality remain.	People have been given wider choice.
Transformationalists	There could be the development of three regional capitalist groups.	Culture is a two-way flow – imports fill less popular slots reflecting consumer choice. People 'localize' cultural messages.

Some of these points were easy to read off from the material available, while others required a more general understanding of the two traditions of thought. What the exercise shows, however, is that theories may be heavily influenced by traditions of thought/ideologies, but they do not neatly follow from them. As you can see, elements of the two ideologies could be found across a range of theories. Had we added conservatism, you would have found strong elements of this in the approaches of both the pessimistic globalists and the inter-nationalists.

 Now please listen to Audio-cassette 7, Side B and read the associated notes. Then return to this point in the workbook.

3 ECONOMIC GLOBALIZATION?

Chapter 3 moves away from a focus on debates about the possible development of a global culture and takes us into questions about economic globalization. In many ways these constitute the heart of the globalization debate as most globalists see economic pressures as the motivating force behind the immense changes that they see taking place to people and to the planet.

The chapter begins by trying to give you some flavour of the variety of ways in which global economic activity is being interpreted, and then presents some examples of the challenges to UK industry and employment caused by global economic competition. This leads into an examination of the competing approaches to economic developments, with a particular focus on the inter-nationalist case.

Chapter 3, 'Economic Globalization?'

- To re-examine the globalization debates with a particular focus on the economy.

- To apply the tests of 'stretching', 'intensification', 'inter-penetration', and the development of a 'global infrastructure' to these debates.

- To identify possible 'winners' and 'losers' from any global developments.

- To explore the inter-nationalist critique of economic globalization.

 Now please read Chapter 3, 'Economic Globalization?' and then return here. You should spend around two-thirds of your time on the chapter and one-third on the workbook.

3.1 Deciphering terminology

Debates about the nature of economic globalization are ongoing, and we hope you found the contents of this chapter both interesting and informative, even though some of the concepts and debates might have been new to you. We have tried to give you working definitions of key terms, so hopefully you have followed the general thrust of what we have written. It is, however, easy to glide over material without taking on board some of its specific points, so compare your understanding with the points below.

WORKBOOK ACTIVITY 3.1

Without looking up the terms in the chapter, briefly note down what you understand by the following terms:

- multinational corporations
- foreign direct investment
- economic liberalism
- GATT.

COMMENT

Multinational corporations (MNCs) are defined by Kelly and Prokhovnik as companies which have some of their productive capacity located in a number of states. This productive capacity may either be acquired by the purchase of shares in existing companies or by new investment in establishing production facilities.

Foreign direct investment (FDI) involves the export of capital by multinational corporations. When an MNC sets up a production plant in another country or purchases shares in one, it is effectively lending money to the country in which it is investing, and that country is therefore borrowing from the MNC's home country.

Economic liberalism involves the belief that individual freedom and economic efficiency are both promoted by increasing the role of the 'free' market in both social and economic policy areas. It emphasizes the value of giving individuals choices and aims to limit government intervention in and regulation of the market.

GATT stands for the General Agreement on Tariffs and Trade and it involved rounds of multinational discussions aimed at reducing taxes and other restrictions on international trade. It was this work which formed the basis for the World Trade Organization (WTO) which was established in 1995.

If you couldn't give answers or you feel your answers were way off beam, don't feel too downcast. We selected these examples because we thought they were quite challenging (as well as being important) and the exercise was meant to illustrate a couple of key points.

In the first place, as we read through the material it is all too easy to lose focus and skate over terms that would otherwise give us problems. In terms of skimming material (see the *Introductory Workbook*) this is quite an understandable and sensible strategy as we are simply trying to get the gist of the argument. However, if the material is central to the points being made in a piece of text then we need to reflect on our understanding of what is being said. We repeat – *at the end of a section, do ask yourself what it was essentially about and question yourself about any terms raised in it.*

The activity also raises one of the key problems of working alone: the possibility of facing difficulties in understanding such terms.

What should you do and not do in such circumstances?

Your answer will clearly depend on the extent of the problem; if there are many problems of understanding then your strategy will be very different from a situation in which there are only two or three points of difficulty. All we can do here is offer you a checklist with some comments:

- **Panic, feel inadequate, cry, provoke an argument with your 'nearest and dearest', etc.** All are understandable reactions, but not realistic solutions, often causing more problems than they can solve. Academic study is hard work, and every student has difficulties understanding material from time to time. You need to develop the confidence to accept this and find ways of living with it.

- **Telephone someone.** Your tutor is an obvious candidate for this, although telephone calls every hour can cause even the most mild-mannered and supportive tutor to develop a nervous tic, or contemplate emigration! Other students are a valuable resource here, and spreading calls around several members of a self-help group can lead to good, friendly working relationships. (On phoning your tutor, see *Workbook 1*, p.61.)

- **Using a dictionary, reference book, etc.** This can be helpful, although as you have probably already noticed, social scientists often use terms in specialized ways that a conventional dictionary may not deal with. Specialist 'Dictionaries of Social Science' exist, but often go deeply into the origins and varied usages of a term. This can leave you even more confused than when you started.

- **Battle away.** Reading the passage(s) many times so that the meaning eventually becomes clear. This can work and is certainly worth trying if the problems are few. However, a great deal of time can be wasted if too many terms are involved. Early in your studies this may be difficult, but it is important to use your judgement here. If a term appears several times or seems to be at the core of the writer's argument, then persevere. If it is only briefly referred to and does not seem to be central, then note it down and delay action on it until it either appears again or you get the opportunity at a tutorial or during a telephone call to seek clarification.

3.2 Extracting the key points from Chapter 3

The chapter highlights the range of different interpretations of global economic developments and then focuses on the globalist, transformationalist and inter-nationalist analyses in turn.

WORKBOOK ACTIVITY 3.2

Either check your existing notes or now make notes under the following headings:

- key points of the globalist interpretations of economic globalization
- key points of transformationalist interpretations
- key points of inter-nationalist interpretations
- 'winners' and 'losers'.

COMMENT

We have chosen a bullet list format for our notes but it would have been equally valuable to have produced a diagrammatic representation, this is very much a matter of personal preference and learning styles. The key is that points should be readily understandable and they should stand out to be easily remembered. Kelly and Prokhovnik offer their own summaries of the three interpretations at the end of their sections, and so we will concentrate here on notes on 'winners' and 'losers'.

WINNERS AND LOSERS FROM GLOBALIZATION

WINNERS

- Quadral Group – economic growth potential for all
- Drug and people traffickers
- MNCs – McDonald's, Microsoft; profits, efficient communication + co-ordination
- Consumers – freedom of choice, easy access to Internet purchases, new commodities
- Computer producers and service providers
- Everyone from the possibilities for peace – Friedman
- Positive globalists – poorer countries – faster technology transfer, reduced corruption and bureaucratic barriers.

<u>LOSERS</u>

- Mander and Barker – ordinary people left homeless and without basic services
- Workers in richer countries – lose out to cheaper labour elsewhere – Jensen cars, Raleigh bikes
- Victims of international drugs trade
- Vulnerable economies – 1997/98 East Asian financial crisis
- Pessimistic globalists – increased pollution, wider gap between rich and poor; less democratic accountability; possibilities for crime and terrorism; less certainty of employment; exploitation of workers
- Women – vulnerability in labour market (Steans), poverty of subsistence farming, cheap labour in manufacturing and service sector, migrant labourers, sex tourism
- Positive globalist view that some states and populations excluded from benefits of global trade through choice or lack of natural resources
- Africa and South America who are failing to have a significant impact on global exports of market-dynamic products.

As you can see, these are very rough notes simply designed to bring points together from different sections of the chapter. To make them more user-friendly we might then re-process them by identifying clearly a 'winner' or 'loser' group, and then attach some details, names of relevant authors etc.

3.3 Practice with numbers

As you have seen, many debates about the significance of global trade and investment involve the interpretation and manipulation of statistics. Here we want to provide the opportunity for you to check your understanding of what is being done and to help you work through a few examples.

Let's begin by looking in general at measuring rates of growth.

When we want to analyse how things change over time we are not interested in the absolute change in the value of, say, exports between two dates, but in the relative significance of the change. For example, the fact that the exports of a firm have increased by £500,000 is much more significant if the firm's previous level of exports was £1,000,000 rather than £10,000,000. In the first case there would be a very large increase of exports compared to a marginal increase in the second case.

	Case 1	Case 2
Previous year's exports (£)	1,000,000	10,000,000
Increase in exports for year in question (£)	500,000	500,000
Exports for year in question (£)	1,500,000	10,500,000

Comparing the change of a value or quantity to its initial size gives valuable information about the speed of change, so we calculate rates of growth.

Using a simple formula we have:

$$\text{rate of growth in exports} = \frac{\text{growth in exports}}{\text{previous level of exports}}$$

The growth in exports simply equals exports in the year in question minus exports in the previous year. So in the first case mentioned above the growth in exports (expressed in pounds) is £1,500,000 − £1,000,000 = £500,000.

The rate of growth expressed as a percentage is therefore:

$$\frac{500,000}{1,000,000} \times \frac{100}{1} = 50 \text{ per cent.}$$

WORKBOOK ACTIVITY 3.3

Now, calculate the rate of growth for the second case mentioned above, noting that the previous value of exports had been £10,000,000.

COMMENT

In this case the growth in exports is again 500,000, obtained by subtracting 10,000,000 from 10,500,000.

So growth in exports = 500,000.

The rate of growth expressed as a percentage is:

$$\text{rate of growth in exports} = \frac{\text{growth in exports}}{\text{previous level of exports}}$$

$$= \frac{500,000}{10,000,000} \times \frac{100}{1} = 5 \text{ per cent.}$$

Now let's look at some calculations on gross domestic product (GDP).

WORKBOOK ACTIVITY 3.4

Work through the following examples and then check your answers with ours in the accompanying comments. Feel free to use a calculator here, and you should certainly do so for question 2 onwards.

1   A country in a particular year had a GDP of £500 million and trade of £100 m. What is the percentage of GDP produced by trade?

2   In 2002 a country exported £455 m worth of goods, and in 2003 £623 m worth of goods. Assuming the value of the pound remained constant, by what percentage had the value of its exports increased?

3   Using the same example and figures, but assuming an inflation rate of the pound of 10 per cent, by what percentage had the value of its exports now increased?

4   In 2003 the GDP of a country was £213,502 m and its merchandise trade was £27,105 m. What was its merchandise trade to GDP ratio, expressed as a percentage?

C O M M E N T

1   The percentage is £100m/£500m × 100 which equals 20 per cent.

2   First,

$$623 - 455 = 168$$

which is the absolute growth in export value.

This increase in export value as a percentage is then:

$$\frac{168}{455} \times 100 = 36.92 \text{ per cent.}$$

3   The percentage increase is now 23.23 per cent.

This is worked out by:

- calculating 10 per cent of 623 = 62.3
- subtracting 62.3 from 623 to find the 2003 exports at 2002 prices = 560.7
- subtracting 455 from 560.7 to find the increased value of exports = 105.7
- dividing 105.7 by 455 and multiplying by 100 = 23.230769
- correcting the figure to two decimal places = 23.23

4   The ratio as a percentage is 12.7 per cent.

The ratio is 27,105:213,502 and the percentage is obtained by multiplying by 100, that is:

$$\frac{27,105}{213,502} \times 100 = 12.695431 \text{ per cent.}$$

The result becomes 12.70 per cent when corrected to two decimal places.

If you haven't tackled anything like this before then you should not be too horrified if you found it quite challenging. If you can't follow the exercise then don't give up – other students will probably be in the same situation so ask your tutor if they will work through some simpler examples with you in a tutorial or on the telephone, etc.

3.4 Applying theories of economic globalization: the story of bananas

From the 1990s there was a significant trade dispute, primarily between the USA and the EU, over special arrangements for their export of bananas to the European market for some former colonies of Britain and France. A range of arguments was put forward by proponents from all sides. Contradictory claims were made about the possible devastation of the livelihoods of thousands of small-scale farmers, the inefficiency and exploitation resulting from European consumers paying too high a price for an inferior product, and threats of the growth of an unfettered drugs trade if farmers were denied the ability to trade as before. The story of bananas does provide a useful case study to bring to life the various analyses of globalization, so let's look briefly at the way the situation evolved.

The Windward Islands of Dominica, St Lucia, Grenada and St Vincent exported bananas to Britain as part of the free-trading arrangements which existed between Britain and her then colonies throughout the world. The French territory of Guadeloupe, also in the Caribbean, and several African states also enjoyed special trading relationships for bananas with their respective colonial powers. When the European Economic Community was established in 1957 and when the UK joined in 1973 special arrangements were made for continued access of products from the Afro-Caribbean and Pacific states (ACP), the designation for the former colonies involved. In 1993 a revised treaty between the EU and the ACP group, while making certain concessions to banana producers in Latin America, continued the preference given in licensing to those importing bananas from the ACP states and imposed tariffs on those from elsewhere. This led to a series of challenges from the USA and a group of central and southern American states that claimed that this constituted discrimination against their produce and marketing companies. Following a prolonged dispute, in April 1999 the WTO authorized the USA to impose a multi-million dollar set of trade sanctions against the EU for its failure to comply with a 1997 ruling against its banana importation policy. The EU reluctantly accepted the decision but continued to look for ways of easing the burden that it would impose on the ACP states.

3.4.1 The Windward Islands' view

Banana export earnings have been extremely important to the Windward Islands, amounting to approximately 70 per cent of export earnings in Dominica and 62 per cent in St Lucia in the late 1980s and early 1990s (Joseph, 1997, p.2). This constituted about a third of their GDP and employed about a half of their active working population. Less directly, this industry fuelled the banking and credit systems, attracted aid to construct vital feeder roads, and produced tax receipts that enabled the governments to invest in improved water and electricity supplies and establish the basis for an expanded tourist industry. Great advances were made in educational provision and constitutional political systems have been established to produce a peaceful and democratic way of life.

In an area that is regularly hit by tropical storms and hurricanes, the banana is vital to the re-establishment of income production as it can be back in production within less than a year of a disaster. The trade does, however, require protection from its competitors, as it is characterized by small-scale production (over 90 per cent of farms are less than ten acres in area), climatic problems mean frequent damage and loss of production, and the terrain makes access to farms difficult. This situation contrasts with that prevailing for its Latin American competitors, where large capital-intensive plantations of thousands of acres of rich soil are operated by multinational corporations.

The EU market and the protection it offered to Windward Islands' banana producers was therefore vital to their well-being and future prospects.

3.4.2 The USA's view

Bananas are the world's largest selling fruit, and the EU provides 40 per cent of the market for them. Latin American producers are the most efficient, providing 75 per cent of world exports, but few went to the EU because of the tariffs and licensing regimes it imposed. This led to European consumers paying far too much for their bananas and guaranteed high profit margins to importers and wholesalers at the consumers' expense, a situation both iniquitous and inefficient. Moreover, the exclusion of Latin American bananas from the European market meant that the supply of them to non-EU countries was artificially high thereby forcing down prices and the incomes of these efficient producers and distributors.

Such a policy has clearly not been in the interests of Latin American producers and European consumers, but it is further argued that it was not in the interests of the Windward Islands themselves. The artificial market locked these economies into dependency on inefficient banana production and to the EU as a market. Producers had no reason to invest in new techniques or improved cultivation practices, and there was no incentive to use the available land, labour and capital in any potentially more productive way. It would have been more effective for the EU to give grants to the governments of the Windward Islands to spend on development projects determined by their own planning policies than to continue wasting resources and harming the free market in this way.

3.4.3 The EU's view

Ostensibly the EU has been committed to defend the interests of former colonies and to enable them to benefit from the European market. Much sympathy has been expressed for the plight of the poor producers and the dire future they face. In 1996 a 'fact-finding mission' of UK MEPs visited the islands and concluded that WTO policies of freeing markets would cause mass poverty, unemployment and instability. This would have a knock-on effect to non-banana producing islands in the area that depended on the purchasing power of people derived from banana sales. It further suggested that there was a real danger that farmers would have to resort to the cultivation of and trade in illegal drugs, and that economic pressures would lead to more illegal immigration to the USA.

However, several points need to be made about this view.

- It has not been universally held within the EU. Windward Islands' bananas were not given equal preference throughout the EU. While they had privileged duty-free access to the UK, and import licenses had to be obtained for non-ACP bananas, until 1993 Germany had a free market for bananas from any source, and other countries such as Ireland and Denmark simply levied 20 per cent duty on all non-ACP bananas.

- From the late 1980s the EU focused more on granting access to EU markets to former communist regimes of eastern Europe than on protecting and enhancing the interests of the ACP states.

- There has been a growing emphasis within EU debates on the value of the competitiveness of the free market, and this has been applied to ACP states as well as to members of the EU itself. Encouragement has been given to the Windward Islands to diversify their economies into tourism and rely less on privileged access to EU markets for bananas.

3.4.4 An inter-nationalist analysis

From what we have seen so far it should be clear that an inter-nationalist analysis would stress a number of key points:

- the self-interested role each state would take on the debate about bananas

- the importance of continuities with older trading patterns

- the interests of multinational companies would be defended by their 'home' states

- the richest and most powerful states would develop their own interests and emerge as the victors

- states would use their power to adapt to the new challenges.

The self-interested nature of the Windward Islands' case in aiming to protect their own sovereignty is clear and unambiguous. They are arguing on both economic and compassionate grounds that their privileged status should have been maintained. Beneath the surface there is a mild threat that there could be unpleasant consequences for the USA in terms of less co-operation against the drugs trade. The fundamental economic and political weakness of the states offered little likelihood of a successful outcome.

The USA's case may appear to be less self-interested as the USA does not itself export any bananas. However, the main banana-exporting companies in Latin America – Chiquita, Del Monte and Dole – are all American owned MNCs and so trade liberalization was certainly in the interests of some of its big corporations. It might also be argued that the post-Cold War situation diminished the significance of the Caribbean to US strategic interests, and so any clout the islands had with Washington disappeared.

The EU case has already been shown to be fragmented, and inter-nationalists would point to the political and economic interests that some European powers have in their former colonies being significant, whilst others have no such interests. The accession to the EU of Austria, Finland and Sweden further weakened the influence of the former colonial powers in shaping EU policies. Even France and the UK have had to balance perceived benefits from the colonial links with those from the accession of new trading partners to the east and the threat of a trade war with the USA.

From such an analysis the decision of the WTO in favour of the critics of the EU/ACP banana agreements and its apparently reluctant acceptance by the EU was inevitable.

WORKBOOK ACTIVITY 3.5

Jot down what you think would have been the main points offered in globalist and transformationalist analyses of the 'story of bananas'?

COMMENT

A globalist analysis would see this story as evidence of the growing and inevitable integration of the world economy, with the economic driving the political and cultural. Then a positive globalist analysis would have:

- stressed the overall benefits of free trade, while recognizing short-term problems for the Windward Islands
- identified longer-term benefits to the Windward Islands in terms of their ability to make more productive use of their land and have less reliance on an artificially supported European market
- seen particular benefits for the Latin American economies and peoples in being able to sell their efficiently-produced bananas in a wider market
- identified this as but one further example of the globalizing economy in enabling producers and consumers to benefit from growing inter-connection
- seen the WTO as a key part of the growing infrastructure facilitating globalization.

A pessimistic globalist would have:

- identified the role of the USA in representing the interests of big business

- stressed the suffering, exploitation, and growth of inequalities that the process is causing

- agreed on the role of the WTO as part of the global infrastructure.

A transformationalist analysis would have:

- recognized the intensification of global interaction involved in the dispute

- identified the continued role for individual state actors, but stressed the new context of international and regional bodies such as the WTO and the EU

- stressed the uncertainty rather than the inevitability involved in the outcome of the dispute

- focused on the evidence of the growing significance of regionalization.

3.5 An evaluation of the inter-nationalist view

The points that inter-nationalists would make in support of their argument would include the following:

- evidence that international trade and investment are not new, and that they could be so affected by the attacks on the World Trade Centre

- evidence that states and regional groupings still retain controls over international links, and most multinational corporations are actually based in particular countries which can control them

- evidence that most companies and consumer markets remain largely national

- evidence that globalization is at most an uneven process, and that its significance remains very much open to debate

- a challenge to the logic of the globalist argument by suggesting it justifies the power of western capitalist states rather than presenting a neutral analyses of what is going on – globalization is being wrongly equated with 'free trade' and the latter is therefore being presented as an inevitable process which poorer countries cannot resist

- a view that it is illogical to see global economic forces as unmanageable – they are to some extent managed and more could be done if there were the will to do so

- taking into account the role that both states and national cultures can have in resisting and adapting pressures towards economic globalization.

If we accept these points we are saying that the inter-nationalist argument is strong because it is supported by the evidence (i.e. it is empirically adequate), it is logical (i.e. it has coherence) and it does take into account a range of factors (i.e. it is comprehensive).

Opponents of the inter-nationalist position would similarly use evidence, question the logic of the argument, and look at the range of factors considered to suggest that it actually has weaknesses as an argument. They might argue that the inter-nationalist argument is weak because of the following points.

- *empirical adequacy:* it tends to ignore or underplay the integration of the world economy – the Asian financial crisis certainly had significant worldwide repercussions. It also may be true that the global activities of multinational corporations could be controlled by particular states, but the evidence suggests that in practice they have a great deal of power to exploit labour, resources and markets in other parts of the world

- *coherence:* a critic might suggest that it is not coherent to treat growing regionalization as an alternative to globalization; it could just as easily be argued that it is simply a stage in the development of the global economy

- *comprehensiveness:* it could be argued that the inter-nationalist argument underplays the globalizing effect of cultural pressures. The inter-nationalist emphasis on the financial value of trade and investment might miss the possible integrating effects of global cultural transmissions.

These points are not raised to establish the accuracy or inaccuracy of the inter-nationalist argument. They are merely an illustration of how a critic of a particular theory would raise questions or doubts about it to suggest that it has significant weaknesses. It is then up to the defenders of the argument to stress the strengths of their view in relation to the weaknesses of those of their opponents.

We will examine Anthony McGrew's views on the *transformationalist* interpretation of globalization and the state in the next section in a similar way.

  Now please listen to Audio-cassette 8, Side A and read the associated notes. Then return to this point in the workbook.

4 POWER SHIFT: FROM NATIONAL GOVERNMENT TO GLOBAL GOVERNANCE?

This chapter focuses on recent developments in the relationship between nation-states and the inter-state system, examining in particular the changing relationships between the United Kingdom and wider international political institutions and influences. It begins by showing how a local event – the death of a young person from an overdose of heroin – can only be understood within a global context.

The chapter highlights the transformationalist position, essentially arguing that while power is no longer primarily located on a national scale, the nation-state continues to have an important role in global governance.

KEY TASKS

Chapter 4, 'Power Shift: From National Government to Global Governance?'

● To answer the question, 'is politics becoming globalized?' and to explore the transformationalist account of globalization.

● To understand the concept of 'global governance'.

● To examine how global governance is being conducted and in whose interests.

● To explore whether we are entering a more unruly or benign world order.

● To critically evaluate the transformationalist argument.

Now read Chapter 4, 'Power Shift: From National Government to Global Governance?' and then return here. You should spend two-thirds of your time on the chapter and one-third on the workbook.

4.1 Extracting the key points from Chapter 4

In this chapter Anthony McGrew is essentially contrasting a past era of global politics dominated by nation-states (what he refers to as the *Westphalian system*) with a developing pattern of politics in the contemporary era that he calls *multi-layered global governance*. In Activity 4.4 in Section 4 of the chapter he asked you to complete a grid which contrasts what he calls the *Westphalian Ideal* with the *Post-Westphalian system*. Before we can begin to evaluate his argument we must first be clear what he means by these concepts and so here we want to make sure you have fully grasped the points he is making.

The Treaty of Westphalia (1648) put an end to the Thirty Years War which was a complex mixture of religious wars, state and empire building, and local class conflicts mainly fought on the territory that is now modern Germany. Without getting involved in the intricacies of the war, it is important to note that it resulted in a defeat for the pretensions of the Emperor of Austria who had hoped to exercise authority over wide swathes of Europe in the name of the 'Holy Roman Emperor' – a title dating back to Charlemagne and the year AD 800. Simultaneously, the war saw the rise of individual princes with the authority to rule over their own small states and to determine the official religions of their populations free from external interference. The system that has come to govern the relationships between these kinds of sovereign states is the Westphalian system.

Five key features of the Westphalian system were identified in Chapter 4:

- territoriality
- sovereignty
- autonomy
- primacy
- anarchy.

WORKBOOK ACTIVITY 4.1

Refer again to Sections 2.1 and 4 of the chapter and then make sure that you have attempted to complete the table in Activity 4.4 which is reproduced below.

	Westphalian Ideal	Post-Westphalian system
Territoriality		

	Westphalian Ideal	Post-Westphalian system
Sovereignty		
Autonomy		
Primacy		
Anarchy		

C O M M E N T _____

Now compare your responses with ours.

	Westphalian Ideal	Post-Westphalian system
Territoriality	Legal and pol. powers of state limited to terr. borders	Borders important – but don't define limits of pol. life and community
Sovereignty	Sov. absolute moral and legal right of states	State power redefined – sov. is a bargaining tool, being bartered, shared and divided
Autonomy	State's right to self-determination and non-interference	State autonomy compromised by interdependence
Primacy	No higher auth. than state – rels. between states depend on consent or force	Primacy, legal and moral challenged
Anarchy	Interstate pol. has dominant power, pol. is free-for-all	Sharing of pol. – McGrew calls it heterarchy, p.163 Erosion of division between dom. and internat.

We have tried to indicate where we would have used abbreviations but have attempted to make them understandable to you by making the words longer than just for personal use. Where we wanted to be sure of the correct spelling of a technical term that we might wish to use in an assignment (namely, heterarchy) we have written it in full and named the source so that we can be sure of the accuracy of the representation.

_____

Anthony McGrew's analysis is built on the *transformationalist* argument, that much more change has taken place in the global sphere than *internationalists* allow; but it rejects the *globalist* view as too extreme. Essentially McGrew is arguing that the state retains an important role in the global system, even if the role has changed dramatically by comparison to the past.

In Section 2.2 he builds up the argument that global politics is having a significant impact on the UK.

W O R K B O O K ACTIVITY 4.2

Make short notes of Section 2.2 and then compare them with ours below.

_____

COMMENT _____

Our notes were:

- 'all areas of human activity' move across terr. boundaries
- nation-states are now 'spaces permeated' by global flows and networks
- power is being internationalized
- G8 - no country can itself stop the drugs trade, or make its own decisions on taxation, the environment, etc
- connects. of gov. depts with international bodies
- 'explosive' growth of internat. bodies - tenfold since 1909
- numerous internat. confs
- growth of internat. NGOs and networks
- the 'institutionalization' of transnational networks
- new centres of authority 'above, below and alongside the state'
- growing 'infrastructure of transnational civil society'
- govts accept wider controls and interests, eg EU, WTO

In Section 2.3 McGrew argues there are institutions of global governance that can be identified at three levels: the *suprastate*, the *substate*, and the *transnational*, with the layer of national government 'sandwiched' between them.

WORKBOOK ACTIVITY 4.3

Read through Section 2.3 and complete the following grid.

	Evidence of institutions of global governance
Suprastate layer	

Evidence of institutions of global governance

Substate
layer

Transnational
layer

COMMENT

We have completed our version of the first row to show again the use of abbreviations, examples, etc.

Evidence of institutions of global governance	
Suprastate layer	Large no. of new internat. bodies, eg WTO. They are new: legal identity with pension schemes etc, wide membership and responsibilities. Emergence of reg. groupings and global alliances. Frequent and substantive summits, ie they take decisions and make policy. Internat. bodies shape domestic policy, eg corp. pun. Conflicts often reflect functions rather than nationality, eg finance.

WORKBOOK ACTIVITY 4.4

Read again through Sections 2.4 and 3.3 of the chapter and note down the key points made in support of the transformationalist case.

COMMENT

Many points could have been noted, ours were:

- state still important but no longer a 'container' – rather a 'space of flows'
- national politics now embedded in wider 'communities of fate'
- shifting balance of power between states and global markets, e.g. East Asian crash
- the transformationalist approach recognizes the importance of individual agents in governance
- 'network' politics resist the forces of global capitalism, thereby leading to elements of 'governance from below', e.g. the 'Stop the MAI' campaign
- important role of experts, at the expense of citizens and politicians, in coping with systemic risks
- the transformationalist position recognizes the significance of state power, corporate power and people power.

To represent the transformationalist argument diagrammatically:

4.2 Evaluating the transformationalist argument

In previous sections of this workbook we have raised questions/doubts about aspects of the arguments presented by Hugh Mackay and Grahame Thompson to show how a critic might begin to evaluate a theory. Now let us have a go at evaluating Anthony McGrew's analysis. Here we will approach McGrew's argument from an *inter-nationalist* position.

Let's start by focusing on the above diagram which summarizes McGrew's transformationalist views and see what questions/doubts we can raise.

WORKBOOK ACTIVITY 4.5

Think carefully about each of the links in the chain in the diagram and try to come up with questions that could be raised about them from the *inter-nationalist* view.

COMMENT

The questions we would raise:

- *Are the problems facing states so much more overwhelming than those in the past?* Major international threats to the existence of states pre-date the Second World War: the great plagues such as the Black Death; invaders such as the Vikings, Napoleon, or Nazi Germany; internal divisions (Royalists vs. Roundheads, nineteenth- and twentieth-century revolutionary movements, Irish nationalism); and international piracy; etc.

- *Are international bodies simply a response to problems or do they merely reflect new ways of pursuing a narrow national interest?* Membership of the World Trade Organization has enabled the USA to push the interests of US owners of banana plantations etc. These international organizations can be said to serve rather than displace the interests of particular states.

- *Are states really adapting their role to such an extent?* They are at least as powerful as ever in policing their populations: they control immigration; they imprison, tax, and mobilize their citizens into armed forces when necessary; and they still take on the responsibilities for the health and education of their populations.

- *Is there really evidence of a new pattern of world governance?* The UN and its agencies can only act when the dominant powers are in agreement; intervention takes place only when the stronger states decide to act in relation to weaker ones (Kosovo, East Timor) and not when the interests of stronger ones are threatened (Russia with regard to Chechnya, China in the case of Tibet). The pattern may not be that states are getting weaker but that new ones are emerging (Croatia, Slovakia and possibly Catalonia, Scotland, etc.). It needs to be stressed that changing boundaries and the creation of new entities has always characterized the Westphalian system (e.g. Belgium, Germany and Italy in the nineteenth century).

So let's take these, and any other questions/doubts we have, and apply the tests of *coherence, empirical adequacy,* and *comprehensiveness* to the transformationalist argument.

Coherence. Again it is possible that answers can be provided by *transformationalists* to these questions, but there are several which can be raised:

- Is it logical to admit that the world campaign against slavery and the slave trade occurred over a century ago and yet still to argue that globalization is new?

- Is it logical to talk about the inability of the state to be sovereign and yet to conclude that 'great inequalities of power, access and influence exist'? Would this not simply support the traditionalist case that at different historical periods there may be different dominant powers?

- Similarly, in terms of NGOs, Anthony McGrew points out that 'many of the poorest and most vulnerable members of the world community have no effective voice at all', does this not again offer support for the traditionalist position?

- Is it logical to assume that states will be willing to accept adapted roles and that new patterns of governance will emerge? Are there unsustainable assumptions of inevitability contained in this argument?

Empirical adequacy. The chapter certainly mobilizes a great deal of evidence in support of its contentions, but there are pieces of evidence that do not fit in:

- Some states have rejected moves towards joining regional groupings, for example Norway and Switzerland rejecting EU membership.

- How representative and significant are the NGOs? What relevance did the Beijing Women's Forum have to the people of Bangladesh and Burkina

Faso, or even to attitudes and behaviour in the Midwest of the USA or Sicily?

- How effective have international organizations, of whatever sort, been in preventing the continued burning of rain forests in Indonesia or Central America?

- Does the evidence offer satisfactory explanations for the rise of nationalism in East Timor, Chechnya or Croatia?

Comprehensiveness. From the points on empirical adequacy we can cast doubts on the approach's ability to explain every example, but in addition we can suggest:

- Does it adequately take into account the strength of the USA, and perhaps a few other states, to dominate international organizations and produce changes that are in its (their) own interests? Is it a model that works for small- and medium-sized states, but not for superpowers?

WORKBOOK ACTIVITY 4.6

Just spend a few minutes considering McGrew's argument from a *globalist* position and try to identify three questions or doubts that its supporters might raise about the *transformationalist* argument. Try to raise a point for each of our three tests of a theory – *coherence, empirical adequacy* and *comprehensiveness*.

COMMENT

Possible points that came to our minds were:

- Membership of the EU has undoubtedly reduced the sovereignty of the British state in terms of the authority of its courts, its ability to place controls on trade. Is it *coherent* then to argue that state power is merely changing rather than being lost?

- Isn't the failure of states to deal with the international drug problem evidence that state power is a thing of the past and so the transformationalist view is not *empirically adequate*?

- Does the transformationalist position adequately take into account the power of MNCs to shape our consumption, attitudes and tastes via the Internet, mass media, advertising, etc? Is it therefore a *comprehensive* argument?

 Now please read *Study Skills Supplement 3: Reading Maps* and listen to the associated Audio-cassette 8, Side B. Then return to this point in the workbook.

5 REFLECTION AND CONSOLIDATION

As in previous blocks of the course, now is the opportunity to pause and consolidate your knowledge and understanding before launching into TMA 04.

 Now please read the Afterword to Book 4. Also watch TV 04 around now (depending on broadcast schedules) and read the associated notes.

Then return to this point in the workbook.

David Held's Afterword to *A Globalizing World?* has, we hope, given you a clearer sense of the debates around the four key questions of this block, as well as some reflection on the role of *structure and agency* in the globalization debate, the *diversity* of responses to globalization and the *uncertainties* it generates.

In Section 5.2 we will be returning to the core questions of the block and in Section 5.3 we look at the use of some of the course themes. But first we want to revisit some aspects of the key skill of the block – *evaluation*.

5.1 Evaluation revisited

You have already covered a lot of ground on evaluation. It is worth reflecting for a moment where in the workbook you have touched on this issue.

- The introduction, which looked at the place of evaluation in the circuit of knowledge and examined three items: *coherence, empirical adequacy* and *comprehensiveness*.

- Section 1.2 which identified four features of globalization which could be used to test propositions about it – these would effectively test the *empirical adequacy* of any theory of globalization.

- Section 1.3 where a grid summarized points raised by globalizers, internationalists and transformationalists.

- Section 2.1 in which contrasts were drawn between the interpretations of the optimistic and pessimistic globalists.

- Section 2.2 which showed how the *coherence* of an argument could be questioned.

- Section 2.4 which showed how social science theories are linked to *larger schools of thought* and *ideologies*.

- Section 3.5 which outlined and offered a critical assessment of the *inter-nationalist* view.

- Section 4.2 which outlined and offered a critical assessment of the *transformationalist* point of view.

In addition to this we want to briefly address two further questions about evaluation (which we will return to in Block 5): the role of *social values* in shaping social science theories (see also *Workbook 3*, Section 2.4) and the ways in which theories can respond to evidence.

WORKBOOK ACTIVITY 5.1

Imagine that you are passing through a shopping precinct and you are hailed by someone selling copies of *The Big Issue*. Note down what you believe your assessment of the situation would be, and also try to think of how someone with different values from yourself might interpret it.

COMMENT _____

Some of us might feel that here is the homeless victim of an unequal and uncaring society who at least deserves the price of the magazine. To others, here is an irresponsible work-shy individual who has 'dropped out' of society, probably indulges in alcohol and/or drug abuse and who should not be allowed to be a virtual beggar on our streets. All of us would see the evidence of a poorly dressed and perhaps sickly-looking individual, but we then, as a result of our values, put a gloss on our interpretation. Therefore we can say that *the observer's values shape the interpretation of the evidence*.

The material we have read in this block has certainly shown that despite diligent and painstaking research, social scientists continue to disagree – in this case globalists vs. inter-nationalists vs. transformationalists. This further illustrates the point that evidence does not 'speak for itself' – it has to be both selected and interpreted, and our 'values' play an important role in these processes.

One important contribution to an understanding of the relationships between theories, evidence and values has been offered by Steven Lukes (1981, p.396) who has suggested that 'theories may be *underdetermined* by data'. By this he means that data or evidence are vital in the establishment of a theory, but data or evidence alone cannot determine a theory's accuracy because values also come into it. To put it another way, any theory is the product of both evidence and values, and consequently two contrasting theories may each fit the evidence. The figure below shows how evidence and values combine to produce a theory, and this, therefore, justifies the social science approach of identifying, collecting and debating evidence to challenge and require a reworking of any theory. This does not mean that the production of evidence will necessarily convert a proponent of one theory to support another, but it may require a reworking of any theory.

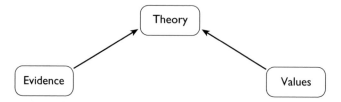

WORKBOOK ACTIVITY 5.2

Look back over the possible points of objection that we raised in Section 3 of this workbook to Bob Kelly and Raia Prokhovnik's inter-nationalist theory. Note down some points on what you think their reaction would be if they were asked to comment.

COMMENT

What is definite is that they wouldn't throw in the towel and declare themselves converts to globalism! They would certainly reject many of the points made – indeed in the chapter itself they have already made a spirited defence of the definitions and measures they used. They might, however, take on board the need to defend their argument against potential critics – they might produce new and more comprehensive examples which the constraints of word limits did not allow in the original text. They might clarify some statements to avoid misunderstanding or misinterpretation. They might even accept that a particular question or point of criticism has some validity and make a marginal change to their argument when they next present it.

Indeed, you know this already at a rather different level from discussions you have had with your friends or loved ones – when they make a telling point in an argument, you don't immediately give in, but you do make a mental note to take on board the point so next time you argue your case you are not vulnerable to it and your argument is consequently stronger.

Do think about this next time you find yourself in a discussion and test whether our prediction of your behaviour is correct.

So that while evidence can disprove or require the reworking of a theory, no amount of evidence can *prove* it to be true. Moreover, we can never know what new evidence will come to light in the future that might totally discredit our apparently sound theory. For example, ancient Egyptians believed that the earth was the centre of the universe because all the visual evidence available to them supported this; the sun and moon and even the stars seemed to travel around it. They could not have predicted the invention of the telescope, etc. which would totally disprove this theory. All we can say is that *the greater the evidence amassed in favour of a particular theory, the stronger that theory will appear to be.*

5.2 Theories of globalization revisited

In Section 1 we began to develop a table of details on the key features of each of the theories of globalization. Here we want you to extend and complete this to provide yourself with a useful summary of the material for use in TMA 04 and also the final assignment of the course.

WORKBOOK ACTIVITY 5.3

Have a go at filling in this grid and compare it with ours below. We suggest you fill in the grid using chapter, section and page numbers from Book 4 so that you have a series of references that you can look up when preparing for TMA 04 or revising for TMA 06.

	Globalists	Inter-nationalists	Transformationalists
What is globalization?			
How significant is contemporary globalization?			

	Globalists	Inter-nationalists	Transformationalists
What is the impact of globalization on the sovereignty and autonomy of nation-states?			
Are there winners and losers in globalization?			
Evidence for			

	Globalists	Inter-nationalists	Transformationalists
Key evidence against			
Place of theory in wider political ideologies			

C O M M E N T

The use of page/section numbers rather than actual points has the benefit that more references can be included. This works with OU courses because you have ownership of the appropriate books and can easily look up references. It would be of much more limited value if you were having to use library books or other borrowed material.

	Globalists	Inter-nationalists	Transformationalists
What is globalization?	Ch. 1, Sects 2.1–3.2 Ch. 1, pp. 22, 24–5 Ch. 3, pp. 90–1	Ch. 1, pp. 23–5 Ch. 3, Sect. 5	Ch. 1, pp. 23–4, 25 Ch. 3, Sect. 4
How significant is contemporary globalization?	Ch. 2, Sect. 2 Ch. 3, Sect. 1	Ch. 2, Sect. 3 Ch. 3, Sect. 5.2	Ch. 2, Sect. 4 Ch. 3, p. 109
What is the impact of globalization on the sovereignty and autonomy of nation-states?	Ch. 4, Sects 2.2, 2.3, 3.2	Ch. 4, Sect. 3.1	Ch. 4, Sects 2.4, 3.3, 4, 5
Are there winners and losers in globalization?	Ch. 1, pp. 22–3 Ch. 2, Sects 2.2, 2.3 Ch. 3, Sects 3.2, 3.3, 3.4 Ch. 4, p. 151	Ch. 3, pp. 119–20 Ch. 4, p. 151	Ch. 3, pp. 106–7 Ch. 4, p. 151
Evidence for	Ch. 1, pp. 15–21 Ch. 1, Sect. 5 Ch. 2, pp. 49–54 Ch. 3, pp. 93–4 Ch. 4, pp. 128–30, 135–48	Ch. 2, pp. 66–71 Ch. 3, Sect. 5.2 Ch. 4, p. 152	Ch. 2, pp. 72–5 Ch. 4, Sects 2.4, 3.3, 4, 5
Key evidence against	Ch. 4, Sect. 3.3	Ch. 1, pp. 15–21 Ch. 2, pp. 49–54 Ch. 4, Sect. 2.2	Ch. 2, Sects 2.3, 3.1, 3.2
Place of theory in wider political ideologies	Ch. 2, pp. 55–7, 63–5 Ch. 3, pp. 95–6, 98–103	Ch. 3, pp. 112–13	

5.3 The course themes revisited

In the introduction to this workbook we noted that despite the change of focus from the United Kingdom to global issues, the issues raised by the course themes remain relevant.

- To what extent are we living in a more *diverse* and/or *uncertain* world?

- How much scope do individual *agents* have to determine their own destinies?

- How important are global *structures* in shaping local and national action?

- In terms of *knowledge and knowing*, how do we study social behaviour and structures and how valid is our evidence?

As we hope you have seen, the questions of a diverse and/or uncertain world are much of what the debates about globalization have been about. Some theorists supporting the globalist view have seen uniformity replacing diversity – global communications, technology, the ubiquitous McDonald's, the removal of barriers to trade, migration, etc. can all be cited. Transformationalists, in particular, argue that the uncertainties over what is taking place mean significant changes to our ways of life, social and economic structures, and the state, but that we don't fully understand or can predict the direction of change. Inter-nationalists provide a direct contrast to this, claiming that little of significance has changed.

Questions of studying society and the validity of evidence have also been at the forefront of what we have been studying. In particular we have looked at quantitative data as evidence and we have examined several forms of data presentation. More than anything else, however, this block of the course has been concerned with how to evaluate conflicting theories.

Perhaps the least up front of the course themes has been *structure and agency*, but debates about structure and agency have been important in informing many of the arguments.

WORKBOOK ACTIVITY 5.4

Look again through your notes on Chapter 1 and mark places where the theme of structure and agency has been relevant.

C O M M E N T

Our notes on this for Chapter 1 are:

AGENCY/STRUCTURE DEBATES

- Feelings of lack of control = poss. of structural changes beyond individual agency

- State structures unable to solve either big or small problems – cannot deliver to their peoples

- Dominance of markets by major players, eg Microsoft
- Creation of global pool of potentially powerless migrant labour
- Pollution caused by others, eg effects of Chernobyl
- Cochrane & Pain suggest globalization provides the structure in which individual agents can influence major institutions
- The super-rich have agency — they can escape into isolation

WORKBOOK ACTIVITY 5.5

Now have a go at filling in this grid.

Structure and agency in Block 4
Chapter 2
Chapter 3

	Structure and agency in Block 4
Chapter 4	
TV 04	

6 ASSESSING BLOCK 4

Your work on the critical evaluation of theories has been leading up to the assignment for this block of the course. In order to help you with this, we want to look at a particular question that is illustrative of the question you will actually be answering and make some comments on how to tackle it.

In approximately 1,500 words, discuss the view that the UK has lost its political and economic sovereignty in a global system.

Although this is not the actual TMA you are being asked to answer this year, as with the earlier specimen assignments, it is essentially the same type of question and will draw upon much of the same material. Therefore, working through the points below should be of direct benefit when you come to face the actual question.

At this point you might find it useful to refer to *Looking Back and Moving On: Writing Essays and Evaluating Theories Booklet* **where valuable general advice on essay writing was given and to consult the study skills index at the back of this workbook for other sources of advice.**

When we look at an essay question we are being asked to answer, several key issues immediately come to mind:

- What type of question is it?
- What length of answer is required?
- What is the central subject matter?
- What terms need defining?
- What are the key arguments and conflicting theories on offer?
- Where will I locate my main sources of evidence?
- What will my basic conclusion be?
- How will I structure my answer?

By asking these at the very outset, we can save a great deal of time and effort in the long run. It means that any reading will be directed to those sections of immediate relevance to the task in hand, and any notes can be collected under the appropriate sub-headings.

Right – so looking at each of these issues we will offer answers for your consideration.

- **What type of question is it?** The key process word here is *discuss* (see the discussion of process words in *Workbook 1*, Section 7.2 and the Appendix in *Workbook 1*). As soon as we see *discuss* in any question we know there will be a debate in which there are several possible answers. Logically, a debate can only take place when there are at least two points of view. From this we know we are expected to show knowledge of those competing views, and there is a requirement to reach a clear conclusion. That does not mean we must totally identify with one view, although we might decide that is the appropriate outcome. It does mean that we should be clear as to our position on the strengths and weaknesses of each view.

- **What length of answer is required?** In this case the question expressly states that approximately 1,500 words are required. This indicates to us that the people who set the question believe that it cannot adequately be answered in a much shorter piece of work. Moreover, the skills that are being tested include careful choice of appropriate material and the succinct expression of analysis of it. Obviously we vary in our styles of writing and it would be wrong to expect us to express ourselves in precisely the same ways, so some flexibility of length is built in. We would generally expect a 10 per cent variation either way to be perfectly acceptable to the marker; and we would certainly expect to be penalized if this particular question were answered in more than 2,000 words.

- **What is the central subject matter?** The question is, in one sense, pretty specific. It indicates that the UK is the focus, so it would therefore be a mistake to bring in lots of material on any other states. It specifies the loss of political and economic sovereignty, suggesting that Chapters 3 and 4 are important, but it must be remembered that the two earlier chapters helped to set up the debates; certainly global culture and communications do have political and economic implications – so relevant points from Chapter 2 should be taken into account and the material on environmental issues in Chapter 1 might also be relevant.

- **What terms need defining?** The key term to deal with here is 'sovereignty', which concerns the moral and legal authority of a state to monopolize the making of laws and the use of force in a particular territory. The reference to 'economic' in addition to 'political' would suggest that some reference to regulations on trade, production, taxation policies, etc. would be particularly relevant, so an indication of this at the outset of the essay would be useful.

- **What are the key arguments and conflicting theories on offer?** Even if you had not studied the book, the very question would indicate that there are at least two possible views – yes, the UK has lost its sovereignty vs. no, it has not. Having read the material, however, you should be able to identify the contrasting views of the so-called globalists, inter-nationalists and transformationalists as constituting the conflicting theories on offer.

- **Where will I locate my main sources of evidence?** As indicated above, Chapters 3 and 4 are central to this question, but Chapters 1 and 2 also have relevance. Consider too if any of the TV and audio tapes etc. provide useful examples. Also, do not neglect what you have already studied in earlier books – the course themes of uncertainty and diversity, structure and agency, and knowledge and knowing link the material from across the course, so a reference to a course theme or to an example linked by it from another block may well be appropriate.

- **What will my basic conclusion be?** This is the key – at the beginning of this workbook we outlined some ways of evaluating theories. In this block you have been presented with three theories, and you need to apply those criteria to decide which theory is the most coherent, comprehensive, etc. As we said above, you do not need to argue that one is perfect and the others wrong, but you should have some clear idea of the strengths and weaknesses of each. In the social sciences there are always several possible answers, so it matters little which answer you plump for – it is the quality of your justification that matters.

- **How will I structure my answer?** This, to some extent, is a personal matter of style, so all we can offer you here is our approach. We would:

  (a) Begin with a short introduction which would map out our intentions – to outline the evidence of loss of sovereignty, describe and examine the three contrasting theories, and to conclude that although it has some deficiencies, theory x seems to be the soundest.

  (b) Outline the evidence of globalization for the UK – global trade patterns, the international media, cultural influences, the drug trade, international organizations, etc.

  (c) Describe in turn each of the three theories, indicating possible strengths and weaknesses. To consider the strengths and weaknesses of each theory you could think about the questions raised by our 'tests'. What kind of evidence supports the theory? Does it cover everything; is it comprehensive? Does it make sense; is it coherent?

  (d) Conclude with reasons why the statement is generally true or untrue.

  These points can be represented in the form of a diagram:

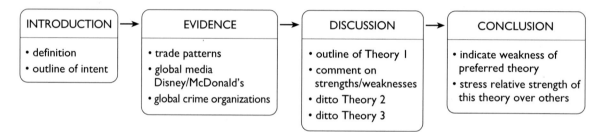

Remember to keep using key words from the question in critical places – for example, the opening sentences of paragraphs – to ensure you are answering the question as set (see especially *Workbook 2*, Section 7.4.3).

 Now turn to the *Assignments Booklet* for TMA 04.

Best of luck!

REFERENCES

Joseph, M.B. (1997) Post-Lomé IV Arrangements Must Mirror the Principles and Instruments of Lomé: A Perspective from the Banana Sectors of the Windward Islands, at http://www.oneworld.org/ecdpm/pubs/wp18_gb.htm (accessed May 2002).

Lukes, S. (1981) 'Fact and theory in the social sciences' in Potter, D. *et al.* (eds) *Society and the Social Sciences: An Introduction*, London, Routledge and Kegan Paul.

ACKNOWLEDGEMENTS

Cover

Image copyright © 1996 PhotoDisc, Inc.

We would like to thank Robert Kelly (jnr) for his help with sections on quantitative data.

STUDY SKILLS INDEX

IWB = *Introductory Workbook*
WB1 = *Workbook 1*
WB2 = *Workbook 2*
WB3 = *Workbook 3*
WB4 = *Workbook 4*
AC7A = *Notes for Audio-cassette 7, Side A*